Contents

(Words printed in **bold italics** are explained in the glossary.)

Making a Link

St Richard's with St Andrew's is a primary school just outside London. When the head teacher, Mr Brooker, was asked if the school would like to be *linked* with a school in Ghana he thought it was a great idea. He decided to ask the children and staff if they agreed.

↑ 'Do you think we should link with a school abroad?'

↑ 'Both schools will make a contribution and enrich each other,' the head teacher says.

School assembly

During assembly, Mr Brooker explained the idea to the rest of the school. He said that it would be a chance for the children in both schools to make new friends. They could send letters and photographs to each other and learn about life in another country.

A great idea!

The more the children thought about it, the more they agreed with Mr Brooker – it was a great idea!

It will help us to learn about living in a different part of the world.

It will be much better than learning from a book.

We can understand them and they can understand us.

We'll be helping children we've never met before.

What next?

Everyone agreed that linking up with a school in Ghana would help them to understand more about being *global citizens*. Now they had to decide what to do next.

Question

Why do you think linking with a school abroad could be a good idea?

It was the organisation Link *Community* Development (LCD) who first contacted Mr Brooker to ask if St Richard's would like to be linked with a school in Ghana. So the first step was to get in touch with them to say 'yes please!' Shortly after, they found out that they had been twinned with Afeghera Primary School.

↑ **Link Community Development supports schools in Ghana, Uganda and South Africa and links them with UK schools. Check out their website at www.lcd.org.uk.**

Afeghera Primary School

The staff and children of Afeghera Primary School had been hoping to be linked with a school in the United Kingdom. They were thrilled when they found out they'd been successful. Their school is in the Bolgatanga district of the Upper East region in Northern Ghana. It is surrounded by farmland and is several kilometres away from the nearest big town.

↑ **Afeghera School is in an isolated place.**

Getting started

An information folder about Afeghera School and a **certificate** arrived at St Richard's by post. At the same time, information about St Richard's was sent to Afeghera. In order to take part St Richard's agreed to raise £250 a year for four years.

Now the children could find out about the school they were going to be linked with.

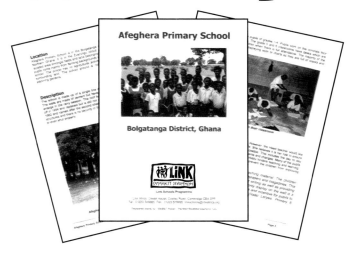

Lots of questions

Straight away, the children wanted to ask all kinds of questions they couldn't find the answers to in the folder. They thought that the Afeghera pupils would have plenty of questions to ask them, too.

What lessons do you have?

How do you get to school?

↑ **The children made a collection of things that would give the children at Afeghera School a lot of information about St Richard's.**

Question

What questions would you like to ask children from a school in another country?

Learning about Ghana

The children got out their atlases and found Ghana on the west coast of Africa, just above the Equator. Afeghera School is in the north, where it is hot and dry and farming can be difficult.

↑ The girls looked for Accra, the capital city of Ghana.

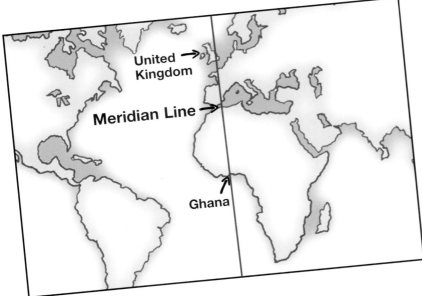

United Kingdom →

Meridian Line →

↑ Ghana

This map shows the position of the Meridian Line.

On the line

The **Meridian Line** (0°) links the United Kingdom with seven other countries – France, Spain, Algeria, Mali, Burkina Faso, Togo and Ghana. So the children found that Ghana and the UK are both on the same line of longitude. They visited the On The Line website to find information and activities about Ghana. Check it out at www.ontheline.org.uk.

I want to know

With their teacher Mr Mathews, the children drew up a short list of the things they already knew about Ghana and Afeghera School, and a much longer list of things they wanted to know.

What can we do to find out more about Ghana and Afeghera School? →

What I know

Ghana is on 0° longitude

On west coast of Africa

Population of 16.5 million

Capital city – Accra

Official language – English

What I want to know

Exactly where is Afeghera School?

What is the school like inside?

What is their school day?

What equipment do they use?

Do the children have a uniform?

What is their religion?

How far do the children travel to school?

How many children are in the school and in each class?

↑ **'That's a picture of playtime.'**

Display

The staff put up a display in the hall of a map of Africa, a big map of Ghana, photographs of the school and newspaper articles. The children can stop as they walk past and find out something new about Ghana and Afeghera School.

Letters and drawings from the pupils and photographs and news about St Richard's were all packed into a parcel, addressed and sent off to Afeghera School. The children waited... and waited... and waited for a reply, but no reply came. At first, they were impatient but then they felt upset.

↑ 'I wonder why they haven't replied.'

No reply!

The postman didn't bring a reply because their parcel never arrived! Post to Afeghera has to be collected from a post box in the nearest town, Bolgatanga, but the system had gone wrong. When the children heard what had happened, they thought about what they had learned.

This is what the children learned about getting in touch with Afeghera School

• Post is not delivered directly to Afeghera School.

• Someone has to make a journey to deliver and collect post.

• There is no electricity so no e-mails can be sent.

• There are no telephones so no phone calls can be made.

Try again

Afeghera School is waiting for a new post box in Bolgatanga. Meanwhile, the best way to make sure post arrives is to deliver it by hand. So the children made up another parcel. This time someone from Link Community Development took it all the way to Ghana.

By Hand.

The Children of Afeghera School,
BOLGATANGA,
UPPER EAST REGION,
GHANA

 There was no need to put stamps on this parcel.

Asking questions

In their letters the children gave lots of information about themselves, and they asked lots of questions.

My family loves pets. We have one dog, one hamster, two cats, three gerbils and ten fish. Do you have any pets?

My ambition is to be in the American air force because of the planes which can reach supersonic speeds, which is very fast. What would you like to be when you grow up?

My hobbies are swimming, playing computer games and hanging out with my friends. What are your hobbies?

My favourite subject is maths because it makes your mind work harder. What is your favourite subject?

Question

Why might the children at Afeghera School have different answers to these questions from the children at St Richard's?

In Touch

Link Community Development sent a group of teachers to Ghana. The ten teachers from all over the UK received a Millennium Award to become global teachers and spend five weeks working in schools in Ghana. One of the team, Jane Fulford, visited Afeghera School and took photographs.

> When I arrived at Afeghera the school was buzzing with noise and excitement.

↑ Jane Fulford (left) is the head teacher of a school in King's Cross, London.

Photographs

The staff and children at Afeghera were very pleased to meet Jane. They showed her all around the school and posed for photographs. They knew the children at St Richard's would be looking at them in a few weeks' time.

↑ The children at St Richard's pored over the photographs from Afeghera.

Latest news

Jane also brought back a letter from Isaac Laryea, the assistant head teacher. He wrote about how the school garden had been flooded in the rainy season and how they are planning to buy cupboards to store their text books.

Dear children...

... The garden became water-logged which made the carrots, the sweet pepper and the groundnuts which were growing well rot, and finally the walls of the garden fell on the carrots which worsened the situation. The community has realised the cause and has put measures in place to prevent any recurrence...

Sincerely yours

I.K. Laryea

↑ **Mr Mathews opened the letter and read it to the children.**

Writing back

Mr Laryea also gave the children a new address to write to. So they got out their pens and paper and started writing straight away.

'Our letters will get there safely this time.' ↗

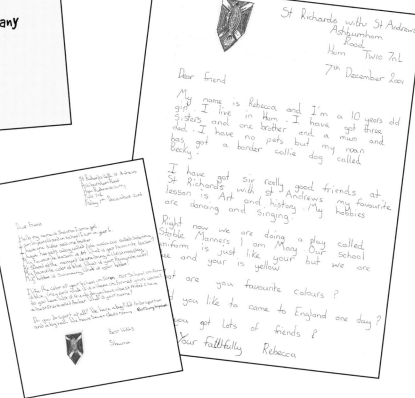

Going to School

The pupils of Afeghera School live in villages like the one in the photograph. Many of their parents are farmers. During harvest and other busy times, some of the children miss school to help with the farming and the chores at home.

↑ The walls and roofs of the village houses are made of mud and wood.

Older children bring the young ones to school. ↑

A long walk

For most of the pupils of St Richard's, the journey to school only takes a few minutes. They either live nearby or travel by car or bus. Afeghera School children walk as far as 4km across fields and farmland to get to school.

The children at St Richard's agree how important it is to go to school however difficult it is to get there.

When we grow up, we can help our children to learn.

It's important to get an education and a good job.

At school, children find out what they are good at.

football crazy

Ghana's football team, the Blackstars, are national heroes. The children play football at break time and dream of playing for the Blackstars. Daniel from St Richard's is football-crazy too. He is planning to send a poster of his favourite team (Manchester United) to Afeghera and ask which teams they support.

Football is popular at playtime. ↑

The tree casts a big, circular shadow. ↑

In the shade

When the hot sun shines down on the playground, the children who don't want to play football find a cool place in the shade of a big tree.

Questions

What do you think is the same about your playtime and playtime at Afeghera?

What do you think is different?

Down to work

 All the schools in the Upper East Region of Ghana have the same yellow and brown uniform. The children at St Richard's spotted the Afeghera School badge on the boy's shirt. They want to know more about it and they are planning to send their own school badge with an explanation of the *symbols*.

The children of Afeghera School wear yellow shirts and brown shorts or skirts. ↗

Symbols

The badge shows St Richard's candle which, according to legend, stayed alight when all other candles blew out during a Candlemas procession. Behind it is the cross of St Andrew.

↓ **There are no desks in grades 1 to 4, so the children work on the floor.**

18

Lessons in English

Lessons in Ghana are given in English even though it is not the language most of the children speak at home. The teacher writes the word 'Literacy' on the blackboard. It's a word St Richard's children know well. They wonder if the lesson will be like their Literacy Hour.

Pictures and posters won't stay up on the walls which get very damp in the rainy season.

← **All the children want to see what is going on.**

Everyone joins in

If word gets out there is an interesting lesson going on, children from other classes crowd round the open windows and join in.

Questions

What languages other than English do children at your school speak at home?

What other language would you like to learn?

Teachers and Equipment

During her visit to Afeghera School, Jane took this picture of the head and assistant head teacher. They sent their warmest greetings to the staff and children at St Richard's.

The head and assistant head teacher ↗ of Afeghera School.

'Tell everyone about the doll.' ↑

Isaac Laryea, the assistant head says:

It is our fervent prayer that the bond between your school and ours continues to grow from strength to strength.

The nursery class

In the nursery, the teacher shows the children a pile of toys. One of the children chooses a toy and talks about it in English.

Equipment

In the staff room, some new equipment has just been delivered. The local carpenter has made a set of Dean's Blocks. The staff admire them and plan how they will use them in their maths lessons.

The local carpenter 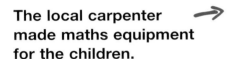 **made maths equipment for the children.**

Sharing ideas

The assistant head sent a set of 'Blue and Red' cards to St Richard's to share ideas with them. The cards are designed to teach addition and subtraction.

Question

Can you think of a teaching aid you could make and send to a school abroad?

Explanation	The blue circles represent positive (+) numbers.

The red squares represent negative (–) numbers.	You have to fill the negatives with the positives to get the answer. So the picture shows: $-3 + 5 = 2$

Global Teachers

When Jane and the other global teachers returned from their trip to Ghana, they met up for a weekend to talk about what they had learned. They had had a wonderful time working in the schools and living in the local communities.

The global teachers were pleased to see each other again.

The global teachers say:

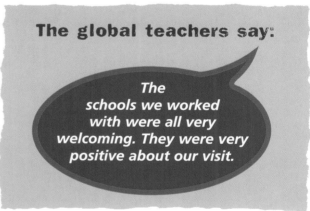

The schools we worked with were all very welcoming. They were very positive about our visit.

Kwame

Kwame Akpokavi is from Ghana. He came to talk to the global teachers about sharing their experiences with their schools. Then he taught them a Ghanaian song and they acted a **traditional** story.

 Kwame talked about art, music and storytelling in Ghana.

Surprise

When Jane got back to her school in London, she had a wonderful surprise. She walked through the doors to see the walls decorated with work the children had been doing about Ghana.

They made their own pots, masks and jewellery. ↓

↑ **The children looked at displays of Ghanaian art.**

What a party!

Jane's school organised a celebration to welcome her home. A Queen Mother from Ghana was invited, the children dressed up in Ghanaian clothes, a king and queen sat under a canopy and everyone sang and danced to the beat of Ghanaian drums.

← **A feast of Ghanaian food was served – rice, fried plantain and spicy chicken.**

The children loved the lively Ghanaian dancing. ↓

A World of Learning

St Richard's have been learning about Ghana too. They invited the Kakatsitsi Master Drummers to visit them and they taught the children to play the drums and dance to the music.

Animal skins are stretched tightly across the hollow drums.

The tooth and the tongue represent friendliness.

Adrinka symbols

King Adrinka of the Ashanti people wore cloth printed with Adrinka symbols. Each symbol has its own special meaning. The children are using Adrinka symbols to make designs for their own prints.

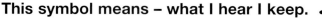

This symbol means – what I hear I keep. →

Oware

Oware is a traditional Ghanaian game of tactics. You have to plan ahead to outwit your opponent. Twelve circles on a sheet of paper and 48 plastic counters are all you need to play Oware. It's a good game for a wet playtime.

↑ **You have to concentrate hard to win Oware.**

The counters 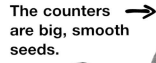 **are big, smooth seeds.**

↖ **This Oware board is decorated with an Adrinka symbol meaning 'Only God'.**

The hands will look like this on the display. The children from Afeghera will fill in the yellow ones. ↑

Joining hands

Some of the children have drawn round both their hands. On one hand they have stuck a photograph on the palm and written an important fact about themselves on each finger. They hope the children from Afeghera will fill in the blank hands and then they can join the hands in a display of friendship.

Raising Money

Raising money can be fun. St Richard's **school council** get together to plan how to reach their target of £250 a year. They come up with a list of ideas and then ask their classes which ones they like best.

↑ 'The *sponsored* swim raised a lot of money last year.'

Ideas for raising money for Afeghera School

A sponsored walk

A sponsored swim

Mufti day

A stall at the Christmas fair

Raffle

Tombola

Lucky dip

Quiz sheets

Christmas stamp competition

A competition was held for the best Christmas stamp design. All the Christmas cards posted in the school postbox had to have a stamp on the envelope. The children send hundreds of cards, so at 1p a stamp they raised quite a lot of money for Afeghera School.

This picture of a little angel was the winner. ↗

Celebration

At harvest time at Afeghera School, every family brings a bowl of nuts, beans or millet to sell at the local market. The money raised goes to the school. But first, the whole community joins in a celebration.

The chiefs and the parents wait for the celebration to begin.

Questions

What does your school celebrate?

Why do you think celebrations can be a good idea?

The musicians play homemade instruments.

friendship

The children, the teachers and the parents of both schools have already learned a great deal from each other. Everyone is looking forward to continuing their friendship and learning even more.

One of the children at St Richard's says:

I'd love to come to Ghana to see what everything looks like, especially your homes and school, and maybe one day you might come to England. One day we might even meet in person.

Glossary

Certificate A certificate is a piece of paper signed by someone in authority to prove that something is official. St Richard's School have a certificate to prove they are officially twinned with Afeghera School.

Community The community is the people who live together. Your local community is all the people who live in your neighbourhood. The global community is all the people who live together on our planet Earth.

Global Global means worldwide. Global teachers travel and work abroad. They share ideas about things that affect everyone in the world.

Global citizen Being a global citizen means understanding that you are a citizen of the world. A global citizen helps to take responsibility for things that concern the whole world.

Link A link is something that joins two things together. When two schools make a link, they join together to make friends and to learn about each other and to give each other support.

Meridian Line The Meridian Line is the 0° line of longitude on the map. It runs from pole to pole and goes through the United Kingdom, France, Spain, Algeria, Mali, Burkina Faso, Togo and Ghana.

School council The school council is a group of pupils and teachers that meet to discuss issues and make decisions. Each class votes for one of their members to represent them on the school council.

Sponsor To sponsor something is to support it with money. For a sponsored swim a sponsor will give a certain amount for every length swum.

Symbol A symbol is a picture that represents something. For example, we often use a picture of a dove as a symbol of peace.

Traditional Something that is traditional has been passed from person to person through the ages. Traditional stories have been told and retold for many years so that they are never forgotten.

Taking Part

Make a link

St Richard's School has made a link with a primary school in Ghana.

Make a link with a school abroad. An organisation like Link Community Development will help you to set it up. Their telephone number is 020 7691 1818.

Invite guests

When St Richard's made the link with Afeghera School, they invited the Kakatsitsi Master Drummers to teach them about music and dance in Ghana.

Invite someone from another country to visit your school to teach you something about it. Ask your families and friends to join in.

Raise money

St Richard's School is planning fund-raising activities to support Afeghera School.

Even if your school isn't linked with another school, you can choose to support a project abroad and then raise money for it.

Be global citizens

The global teachers talk to their schools and their community about things that concern the whole world.

Caring for the environment is one way you can be good global citizens. Discuss ways your school can help to make a difference to the world.

Index

First published in 2002 by
Franklin Watts
96 Leonard Street
LONDON
EC2A 4XD

Franklin Watts Australia
56 O'Riordan Street
Alexandria
NSW 2015

ISBN: 0 7496 4366 8
Dewey Decimal Classification 371.3
A CIP catalogue reference for this book is available from the British Library.

Printed in Malaysia

Editor: Kate Banham
Designer: Joelle Wheelwright
Art Direction: Peter Scoulding
Photography: Chris Fairclough

Acknowledgements
The publishers would like to thank the staff and pupils of St Richard's with St Andrew's Primary School, Ham, Richmond, Surrey, and of Afeghera School, Bolgatanga, Ghana for their help in the production of this book. We would also like to thank Kate Griffin and Link Community Development, and Jane Fulford and the other global teachers. The Global Teacher Millennium Awards are funded by the Millennium Commission. Extra photographs were kindly supplied by the following:
Jane Fulford: (front cover top left), pages 14, 16 (top), 17 (bottom), 18 (top), 19–21 and 27.
Barry Harding: page 16 (bottom).
Sally Hewitt: pages 15, 22, 23 and 25 (centre).
Link Community Development: pages 8 and 18 (bottom).
St Richard's with St Andrew's Primary School: page 24 (top).
Alan Williams: page 17 (top).

370

TAKING

PART

Twinned Schools

by Sally Hewitt

Photographs by Chris Fairclough